The Kingfisher Book of

Family
Poems

KINGFISHER
a Houghton Mifflin Company imprint
215 Park Avenue South
New York, New York 10003
www.houghtonmifflinbooks.com

First published in hardcover by Kingfisher in 2003
10 9 8 7 6 5 4 3 2 1

LIBRARY OF CONGRESS CATALOGING-IN-PUBLICATION DATA has been applied for.

ISBN 0-7534-5557-9

Printed in Hong Kong
1TR/1202/PROSP/BS(FR)/140WF(W)

The Kingfisher Book of

Family Poems

Selected by

Belinda Hollyer

Illustrated by

Holly Swain

KINGFISHER
NEW YORK

To Brenda and Jane:
always loved, never stewed (see page 95)—**B. H.**

To my family—**H. S.**

Contents

EVERYBODY SAYS

Everybody says
I look just like my mother.
Everybody says
I'm the image of Aunt Bee.
Everybody says
My nose is like my father's
But *I* want to look like *ME*!

DOROTHY ALDIS

FAMILY TREE

My sister's mother's
husband's brother's
nephew's sister's
brother's . . . ME!

LINDSAY MacRAE

I AM THE YOUNGEST

I Am The Youngest   So They Call
                        Me   All
                        Day Long

My Name Is Rebecca At Breakfast
                            Time
                Becky By Lunch
                        But
        Becka
        Beck
        Beck Come
                Wash   Your
                        Neck
        Is Daddy's Supper
                Song

                        I Like My Real
                        Name   Short
                        And   My Hair
                        Real   Long
I Am The Youngest   And I Belong

ARNOLD ADOFF

18

FACE IT

My nose belongs
to Guangdong, China—
short and round, a Jang family nose.

My eyes belong
to Alsace, France—
wide like Grandmother Hemmerling's.

But my mouth, my big-talking mouth, belongs
to me, alone.

JANET S. WONG

THEY CHOSE ME

I have two mothers,
My birth mother and my Mum.
I have two fathers,
My blood father and my Dad.

But of all the babies born
In the whole wide world,
My Mum and Dad chose me.

I have two days,
My Birthday and my Chosen Day.
I get two cakes
And have my friends to tea.

But of all the babies born
In the whole wide world,
My Mum and Dad chose me.

I am the one,
The child they went to find,
I am the one
To make their family,

For of all the babies born
In the whole wide world,
My Mum and Dad chose me.

JAMILA GAVIN

SCHOOL CONCERT

My family was the very proudest.
They said my singing was the loudest.

MARCHETTE CHUTE

A MUSICAL FAMILY

I can play the piano
I am nearly three.
I can play the long white note
That Mum calls Middle C.

Dad can play the clarinet.
My sister plays the fiddle,
But I'm the one who hits the piano
Slap bang in the middle.

JOHN MOLE

KISSES!

Last week
my face was smothered in kisses.
YES – **KISSES!**
First there was the **dribbly-wibbly kiss**
when Mum slurped all over me
like an eight-mouthed octopus.
   ("There's my favourite boy!")
Then there was the **lipstick-redstick kiss**
when my aunty's rosy lips
painted themselves on my cheeks.
   ("Isn't he so handsome!")
Next came the **flutter-eye, butterfly kiss**
when my girlfriend smoochy-cooched
and fluttered her eyelashes at the same time.
   ("OOOOOOOOH!")
After that there was the **soggy-doggy kiss**
when our pet Labrador Sally
tried to lick my face off. ("Slop! Slop! Woof!")
Following that there was the **"watch out here I come"
   miss-kiss**
when my little sister aimed for me
but missed and kissed the cat instead.
   ("UUUUUUUUURGH!")
Then there was the **spectacular-Dracula kiss**
when my cousin Isabel leapt from behind the
   shower curtain
and attacked my neck. ("AAAAAAAAAAGH – suck!")

Of course, there was the **"sssssssssh don't tell anyone"
    self-kiss**
when I looked in the bathroom mirror
and kissed myself. (Once was enough!)
But the unbeatable, second to none, zing-dinger of a kiss
came from Gran.
It was a lip-sucking, cheek-plucking, Donald Duckling
SMACKEROONY OF A KISS. (She'd forgotten to put
    her teeth in!)

IAN SOUTER

MUM DAD AND ME

My parents grew among palmtrees,
in sunshine strong and clear.
I grow in weather that's pale,
misty, watery or plain cold,
around back streets of London.

Dad swam in warm sea, at my age.
I swim in a roofed pool.
Mum – she still doesn't swim.

Mum went to an open village market
at my age. I go to a covered
arcade one with her now.
Dad works most Saturdays.

At my age Dad played
cricket with friends.
Mum helped her mum, or talked
shouting halfway up a hill.
Now I read or talk on the phone.

With her friends Mum's mum washed
clothes on a river-stone. Now
washing-machine washes our clothes.
We save time to eat to TV,
never speaking.

My dad longed for a freedom in Jamaica.
I want a greater freedom.
Mum prays for us, always.

Mum goes to church
some evenings and Sundays.
I go to the library.
Dad goes for his darts at the local.

Mum walked everywhere, at my age.
Dad rode a donkey.
Now I take a bus
or catch the underground train.

JAMES BERRY

NEWCOMERS

My father came to England
from another country
My father's mother came to England
from another country
but my father's father
stayed behind.

So my dad had no dad here
and I never saw him at all.

One day in spring
some things arrived:
a few old papers,
a few old photos
and — oh yes —
a hulky bulky thick checked jacket
that belonged to the man
I would have called "Grandad".
The Man Who Stayed Behind.

But I kept that jacket
and I wore it
and I wore it
and I wore it
till it wore right through
at the back.

MICHAEL ROSEN

SEEING ALL MY FAMILY

Seeing all my family
together
at special occasions
is a brilliant firework show
going off.

Grandma is a sparkler,
Grandad is golden rain
making us brighter.
My cousins
are Catherine Wheels.
My dad is a banger
because he always talks too loud.
The best one of all
that lights up the sky
so everyone stares
is my mum
the incredible blast of sparkle
the rocket.

Every time we meet,
it always has the same effect
our family firework show.

CLAIRE SALAMA

NERISSA

Her daddy's out of work
and her mama's sick in bed
Nerissa tries to think of things
to make them glad
she can't bring dinner
like the neighbors do
she can't mend the hole
in her daddy's shoe
but she's a big help
when she tickles her folks
by telling them the best old
bedtime jokes

ELOISE GREENFIELD

WILL YOU BE MY FAMILY?

Will you take my picture?
Will you take my side?
Will you take the pain away
I've tried so hard to hide?

Will you watch me play in goal
In foul or freezing weather?
Could we spend all Christmases
And holidays together?

Will you pack a lunch for me?
Sometimes hold my hand?
Can we be just ordinary?
Do you understand?

When I throw a tantrum
Will you promise not to pack?
If I learn to love you
Will you try to love me back?

Will we see the funny side?
Laugh when times get tough?
We will be a family
That will be enough.

LINDSAY MACRAE

Introduction

A family can mean many different things. To you, it might just mean you and your mom and dad. Or it might mean you and your mom and your two brothers; and your dad, who doesn't live with you; and your stepfather and stepsister; and some aunts and uncles and cousins; and a friend of your mom's whom you call auntie (although she's not related to you); and your grandma and grandpa across the street; and your other grandparents in Argentina, whom you've never met—oh, and Bubble the goldfish, too.

Whatever it means to you, family is very important. Everyone wants to have a family. (At times you might not want the family you have—but that's another story.) Your family knows you better than anyone else. They understand you and love you no matter what—however much you argue or however often you see (or don't see) each other. Families are forever.

Growing up as part of a family is something people do all around the world, but no one's home, no one's life, and especially no one's family is exactly like anyone else's. Everyone feels differently about their own family. Your little brother might drive you crazy, and your big sister might tease you; you might hate being kissed by your great aunt or wish you didn't have to play with your cousins. On the other hand maybe your brothers and sisters are angels, your great aunt's a superstar, and you just wish you had some cousins to play with . . .

Living in a family gives you a treasure chest of love and laughter and a lifetime of memories.

The 159 poems in this collection explore just about every family situation. There are poems about celebrations and about remembering sad times. There are poems about a grandmother's tired old legs, about a new baby sister, and about the awfulness of your mother wiping your face in front of your friends. There are poems about being the youngest in the family, about being an only child, and about being adopted. There's a poem about having to eat muesli for breakfast, another about what your pet hamster does all day, and even one about watching your dad cut his toenails.

From the family that's like a comforting quilt in the first poem to the outlandish family in the last poem, there is something here for everyone. I hope you find at least one poem that makes you say *Oh yes! that's like my family!*—and I think you will.

BELINDA HOLLYER
MARCH 2003

Family quilt

QUILT

Our family
is a quilt

of odd remnants
patched together

in a strange
pattern,

threads fraying,
fabric wearing thin—

but made to keep
its warmth

even in bitter
cold.

JANET S. WONG

TWO PEOPLE

She reads the paper,
while he turns on TV;
she likes the mountains,
he craves the sea.

He'd rather drive,
she'll take the plane;
he waits for sunshine;
she walks in the rain.

He gulps down cold drinks,
she sips at hot;
he asks, "Why go?"
She asks, "Why not?"

In just about everything
they disagree,
but they love one another
and they both love me.

EVE MERRIAM

I LUV ME MUDDER

I luv me mudder an me mudder luvs me
    We cum so far from over de sea,
We heard dat de streets were paved wid gold
    Sometimes it's hot, sometimes it's cold,
I luv me mudder an me mudder luvs me
    We try fe live in harmony
Yu might know her as Valerie
    But to me she's just my mummy.

She shouts at me daddy so loud sometime
    She's always been a friend of mine
She's always doing de best she can
    She works so hard down ina Englan,
She's always singin sum kinda song
    She has big muscles an she very, very strong,
She likes pussycats an she luvs cashew nuts
    An she don't bother wid no if an buts.

I luv me mudder an me mudder luvs me
    We come so far from over de sea,
We heard dat de streets were paved wid gold
    Sometimes it's hot, sometimes it's cold,
I luv her and whatever we do
    Dis is a luv I know is true,
My people, I'm talking to yu
    Me and my mudder we luv yu too.

BENJAMIN ZEPHANIAH

HUMAN AFFECTION

Mother, I love you so.
Said the child, I love you more than I know.
She laid her head on her mother's arm,
And the love between them kept them warm.

STEVIE SMITH

GROWING

Today
you may be small.
But one day
you'll be tall,
like me,
maybe taller.
You won't
fit into your bed.
Your hat
won't fit on your head.
Your feet
will fill up the floor.
You'll have to bend down
to come through the door.
You'll be able to reach
to the highest shelf,
(and I can't do that now,
myself).
Out in the country
the tallest trees
will scratch your ankles
and tickle your knees.
Up in the clouds,
yes, way up there,
the eagles will nest
in your craggy hair.

But they'd better soon find
a safer place
because soon your head
will be up in space.

So I hope you won't be too proud
to bend down
and say hello
to your old home-town.
And I hope it won't drive you
utterly mad
to visit your tiny
Mum and Dad.

TONY MITTON

FATHER, MOTHER, AND ME

Father, Mother, and Me,
   Sister and Auntie say
All the people like us are We,
   And every one else is They.

RUDYARD KIPLING

Mama look like Christmas

SQUEEZES

We love to squeeze bananas,
We love to squeeze ripe plums,
And when they are feeling sad
We love to squeeze our mums.

BRIAN PATTEN

MY NATURAL MAMA

my natural mama
is gingerbread
all brown and
spicy sweet.
some mamas are rye
or white or
golden wheat
but my natural mama
is gingerbread,
brown and spicy sweet.

LUCILLE CLIFTON

WHA ME MUDDER DO

Mek me tell you wha me Mudder do
wha me mudder do
wha me mudder do

Me mudder pound plantain mek fufu
Me mudder catch crab mek calaloo stew

    Mek me tell you wha me mudder do
    wha me mudder do
    wha me mudder do

    Me mudder beat hammer
    Me mudder turn screw
    she paint chair red
    then she paint it blue

    Mek me tell you wha me mudder do
    wha me mudder do
    wha me mudder do

Me mudder chase bad-cow
with one "Shoo"
she paddle down river
in she own canoe
Ain't have nothing
dat me mudder can't do
Ain't have nothing
dat me mudder can't do

Mek me tell you

GRACE NICHOLS

BREAKFAST

Mum makes me eat muesli.
I always try a "no" but

    she just says
    it's good for me to
    eat a bowl of
    oats and bran that's
    full of fruit, nutritious nuts and
    vitamins B, C and D.

It helps your insides go.

Mum makes Dad eat muesli.
He always pulls a face but

    she just says
    it's good for him he's
    overweight and
    not that young and
    ought to think about his heart and
    throw away the frying pan.

You'll get used to the taste.

This morning very early before the world was up,
strange sounds from the kitchen
something sizzling, something hot.

So I
crept down
quick and quiet
on ten tip-toes to
find out

Who was secretively scoffing
eggs and bacon?

It was Mum!

DANIELLE SENSIER

THE PAINTING LESSON

"What's THAT dear?"
asked the new teacher.

"It's Mummy," I replied.

"But mums aren't green and orange!
You really haven't TRIED.
You don't just paint in SPLODGES
– You're old enough to know
You need to THINK before you work . . .
Now – have another go."

She helped me draw two arms and legs,
A face with sickly smile,
A rounded body, dark brown hair,
A hat – and, in a while,
She stood back (with her face bright pink):
"That's SO much better – don't you think?"

But she turned white
At ten to three
When an orange-green blob
Collected me.

"Hi, Mum!"

TREVOR HARVEY

MAMA

Mama gone to market
with the figs upon her head.
She wearin' her soft blue
dress for selling
with the fish 'round the hem.
Her hair is plaited neatly
in two long straps of black.
She walkin' tall in sandals
with the bamboo beads intact.
Mama look like Christmas
with red sorrel behind her ears.
She balance her wicker basket
like the Star of Bethlehem.

LYNN JOSEPH

I TOLD YOU SO

My mother never says, "I told you so."
She doesn't believe in it.
She calls it "rubbing salt in the wound."
But sometimes, her silences are so loud
That we wish she'd give in, for once,
And get it off our minds.

JEAN LITTLE

MUM DOESN'T LIVE
WITH US ANY MORE

There's a start of the day
Where Mum ought to be.

There's a silent breakfast
Where Mum ought to be.

There's a gate to wave at
Where Mum ought to be.

There's a coming home at four
Where Mum ought to be.

There's an empty kitchen
Where Mum ought to be.

There's an end of the day
Where Mum ought to be.

JOHN COLDWELL

VICTORIA'S POEM

Send me upstairs without any tea,
refuse me a plaster to stick on my knee.

Make me kiss Grandpa who smells of his pipe,
make me eat beetroot, make me eat tripe.

Throw all my best dolls into the river.
Make me eat bacon and onions – with liver.

Tell Mr Allan I've been a bad girl,
rename me Nellie, rename me Pearl.

But don't, even if
the world suddenly ends
ever again,
Mother,
wipe my face with a tissue
in front of my friends.

FRED SEDGWICK

MILLICENT'S MOTHER

Millie buttons her coat, gives her mother a kiss,
Then Millicent's mother says something like this:
"Millie, take your umbrella in case there's a storm,
And be sure to wear mittens to keep your hands warm,
And, since it may snow, take your snowshoes and parka,
And pack your big flashlight in case it gets dark-a.
This bicycle pump will help fix a flat tire,
This fire extinguisher puts out a fire,
And take this roast turkey, you may need a snack,
This map and this compass will help you get back,
And take your galoshes, there may be some mud,
And your scuba-dive outfit in case there's a flood,
And in case you get bored, take your toys in your wagon,
And please wear your armor, in case there's a dragon."
"Oh, Mommy!" says Millie. "I don't need all that!"
"Okay," says her mother. "But wear a warm hat."

JEFF MOSS

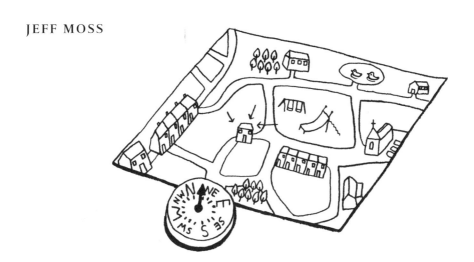

THE SPEAK MUM SPEAKS

the speak Mum speaks
when she's on the phone
I asked her one time
where it comes from
she says it's the speak
of her friends from home

the speak Mum speaks
like floating and laughing
and the words are bubbling
whispering hurrying
she says it's the speak
of where she comes from

the speak Mum speaks
like singing and dancing
like friends holding hands
going out to playtime
like a playground
with everyone jumping

I sit small and say nothing
I listen and listen
to the speak Mum speaks
flashing and shining
like jewel diamonds
and I want some

HELEN DUNMORE

STEPMOTHER

My stepmother
    is really nice.
She ought to wear
    a label.
I don't come in
    with a latch key, now –
my tea is on
    the table.
She doesn't nag at me
    or shout.
I often hear her
    singing.
I'm glad my dad
    had wedding bells –
and I hope
    they go on ringing.

Stepmothers
    in fairy tales
are hard and cold
    as iron.
There isn't a lie
    they wouldn't tell,
or a trick
    they wouldn't try on.
But MY stepmother's
    warm and true;
she's kind, and cool,
    and clever –
Yes! I've a *wicked*
    stepmother –
and I hope she stays
    for ever!

JEAN KENWARD

HAPPY BIRTHDAY, MOTHER DEAREST

Happy birthday, Mother dearest,
we made breakfast just for you,
a watermelon omelette,
and a dish of popcorn too,
a cup of milk and sugar,
and a slice of blackened toast,
happy birthday, Mother dearest,
you're the one we love the most.

JACK PRELUTSKY

They'll be sorry!

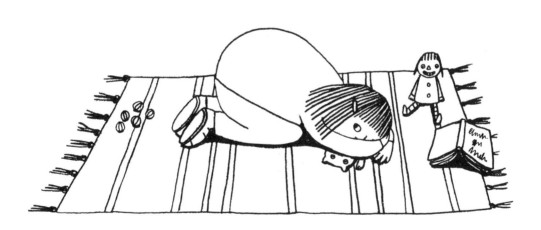

BILLY IS BLOWING HIS TRUMPET

Billy is blowing his trumpet;
Bertie is banging a tin;
Betty is crying for Mummy
And Bob has pricked Ben with a pin.
Baby is crying out loudly;
He's out on the lawn in his pram.
I am the only one silent
And I've eaten all of the jam.

ANON

ASK MUMMY ASK DADDY

When I ask Daddy
Daddy says ask Mummy

When I ask Mummy
Mummy says ask Daddy.
I don't know where to go.

Better ask my teddy
he never says no.

JOHN AGARD

GO AWAY

Somehow I'm always
                    in the way.
I'm always sent somewhere
                              to play,
Or told to go and watch tv.
Is it them?
            Or is it me?

LINDAMICHELLEBARON

PITY YOUR PARENTS

My Gran once said, "Remember, lad,
You must be kind to Mum and Dad:
They do the best they can, poor things;
Angels they aren't, they don't have wings."

It must be quite a strain to be
Responsible for kids like me.
I'm sure it drives them up the wall,
Pretending that they know it all.

"Your room's a mess" – "Don't tease the cat" –
"I've warned you – don't use words like that!"
They're never wrong, they're always right.

No wonder they can't sleep at night.

ROGER WODDIS

THE PARENT

Children aren't happy with nothing to ignore,
And that's what parents were created for.

OGDEN NASH

GRANDPA IS ASHAMED

A child need not be very clever
To learn that "Later, dear" means "Never."

OGDEN NASH

THE RUNAWAY

I made peanut butter sandwiches.
I didn't leave a mess.
I packed my shell collection
and my velvet party dress,
the locket Grandma gave me
and two pairs of extra socks,
my brother's boy scout flashlight
and some magic wishing rocks.

Oh, they'll be so sorry.
Oh, they'll be so sad,
when they start to realize
what a nifty kid they had.

I'd really like to be here
when they wring their hands and say,
"We drove the poor child to it.
She finally ran away."

If I peeked through the window
I'd see them dressed in black,
and hear them sob and softly sigh,
"Come back, dear child! Come back!"

The house will be so quiet.
My room will be so clean.
And they'll be oh so sorry
that they were oh so mean!

BOBBI KATZ

61

DEAR MUM,

while you were out
a cup went and broke itself,
a crack appeared in the blue vase
your great-great grandad
brought back from China.
Somehow, without me even turning on the tap,
the sink mysteriously overflowed.
A strange jam-stain,
about the size of a boy's hand,
appeared on the kitchen wall.
I don't think we will ever discover
exactly how the cat
managed to turn on the washing-machine
(specially from the inside),
or how the self-raising flour
managed to self-raise.
I can tell you I was scared when,
as if by magic,
a series of muddy footprints
appeared on the new white carpet.
I was being good
(honest)
but I think the house is haunted so,
knowing you're going to have a fit,
I've gone over to Gran's for a bit.

BRIAN PATTEN

MYSTERY

CRASH!!!
DAD: What was that noise?
SON: The bowl. I've broken the bowl.
MUM: What bowl?
SON: The one with lines on.
DAD: How did you break it?
SON: I was balancing it on my head.
DAD: The boy's mad.
MUM: How else is he going to practise?
DAD: Why were you balancing it on your head?
SON: I was pretending it was a hat.
DAD: Why do you need to practise pretending a bowl
    is a hat?
SON: (NO ANSWER)

MICHAEL ROSEN

SOAP

Just look at those hands!
Did you actually think
That the dirt would come off, my daughter,
By wiggling your fingers
Around in the sink
And slapping the top of the water?

Just look at your face!
Did you really suppose
Those smudges would all disappear
With a dab at your chin
And the tip of your nose
And a rub on the back of one ear?

You tell me your face
And your fingers are *clean*?
Do you think your old Dad is a dope?
Let's try it again
With a different routine.
This time we'll make use of the soap!

MARTIN GARDNER

MUM'LL BE COMING HOME TODAY

Mum'll be coming home today.
It's three weeks she's been away.
When Dad's alone
all we eat
is cold meat
which I don't like
and he burns the toast I want just-brown
and I hate taking the ash-can down.

He's mended the door
from the little fight
on Thursday night
so it doesn't show
and can we have grilled tomatoes
Spanish onions and roast potatoes
and will you sing me "I'll never more roam"
when I'm in bed, when you've come home.

MICHAEL ROSEN

MY BABY BROTHER

My baby brother is a killer
He pulls my hair and throws me down
on the floor and spits in my face and
squeezes my nose and takes off my
glasses and then tries them on and
throws them away and he jumps on
my stomach and he bites my toes and
he counts my fingers and my mother
says, "Ian, get off the floor."

IAN AITKEN

YOU MIGHT AS WELL . . .

Small brothers blame you;
Big ones skulk;
Mothers shame you;
Sisters sulk.
Dads won't budge
Unless you shove 'em.
But they're family;
You might as well love 'em.

LINDSAY MacRAE

EMMA HACKETT'S NEWSBOOK

Last night my mum
Got really mad
And threw a jam tart
At my dad.
Dad lost his temper
Then with mother,
Threw one at her
And hit my brother.
My brother thought
It was my sister,
Threw two at her
But somehow missed her.
My sister,
She is only three,
Hurled four at him
And one at me!

I said I wouldn't
Stand for that,
Aimed one at her
And hit the cat.
The cat jumped up
Like he'd been shot,
And landed
In the baby's cot.
The baby —
Quietly sucking his thumb —
Then started howling
For my mum.
At which my mum
Got *really* mad
And threw a Swiss roll
At my dad.

ALLAN AHLBERG

I CAN HEAR THE TREES WHISPERING

I can hear the trees whispering
    the cats purring
    the dogs barking
No wonder I can't get to sleep.

I can hear my dad in a rage
tearing up a page into little bits
while my mother sits crying
No wonder I can't get to sleep.

MARSHA PROVIDENCE

THERE ARE FOUR CHAIRS
ROUND THE TABLE

There are four chairs round the table,
Where we sit down for our tea.
But now we only set places
For Mum, for Terry and me.

We don't chatter any more
About what we did in the day.
Terry and I eat quickly,
Then we both go out to play.

Mum doesn't smile like she used to.
Often, she just sits and sighs.
Sometimes, I know from the smudges,
That while we are out she cries.

JOHN FOSTER

DINNERTIME

Slowly slowly
glides his hand beneath the table.
I see his fingers
clutch a corner of my napkin.
Gently gently
slides the napkin off my lap.
I pounce.
Gotcha!

You two better stop that.
Stop what?
Stop whatever it is you're doing.
We're not doing anything.
Then stop whatever it is you're not doing.
Geez.

Slowly slowly
glides my hand beneath the table.
My fingers grope.
Gently gently
slides the napkin. . . .

RICHARD J. MARGOLIS

SOMETIMES

Sometimes I share things,
And everyone says
"Isn't it lovely? Isn't it fine?"

I give my little brother
Half my ice cream cone
And let him play
With toys that are mine.

But today
I don't feel like sharing.
Today
I want to be left alone.
Today
I don't want to give my little brother
A single thing except
A shove.

EVE MERRIAM

HELP!

Firemen, firemen!
State police!
Victor's locked in Pop's valise!
Robert's eating kitty litter!
Doctor!
        Lawyer!
                Baby-sitter!

X. J. KENNEDY

In Daddy's arms

MY DADDY DANCES TAPSTEP

Roger's Daddy's clever
Daisy's flies a plane
Michael's does computers
And has a house in Spain.
Lucy's goes to London
He stays there every week . . .
    But my Daddy has an earring
        and lovely dancing feet.

He hasn't got a briefcase
He hasn't got a phone
He hasn't got a mortgage
And we haven't got a home.
He hasn't got a fax machine
We haven't got a car
    But he can dance and fiddle
        And my Daddy is
        A Star.

PETER DIXON

DAD

Dad is the dancing-man,
The laughing-bear, the prickle-chin,
The tickle-fingers, jungle-roars,
Bucking bronco, rocking-horse,
The helicopter roundabout,
The beat-the-wind at swing-and-shout,
Goal-post, scary-ghost,
Climbing-Jack, humpty-back.

But sometimes he's
A go-away-please!
A snorey-snarl, a sprawly slump.
A yawny mouth, a sleeping lump,

And I'm a kite without a string
Waiting for Dad to dance again.

BERLIE DOHERTY

I WISH MY FATHER WOULDN'T TRY
TO FIX THINGS ANYMORE

My father's listed everything
he's planning to repair,
I hope he won't attempt it,
for the talent isn't there,
he tinkered with the toaster
when the toaster wouldn't pop,
now we keep it disconnected,
but we cannot make it stop.

He fiddled with the blender,
and he took a clock apart,
the clock is running backward,
and the blender will not start,
every windowpane he's puttied
now admits the slightest breeze,
and he's half destroyed the furnace,
if we're lucky, we won't freeze.

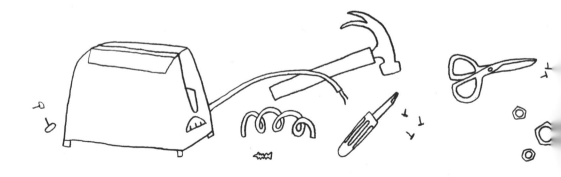

The TV set was working,
yet he thought he'd poke around,
now the picture's out of focus,
and there isn't any sound,
there's a faucet in the basement
that had dripped one drop all year,
since he fixed it, we can't find it
without wearing scuba gear.

I wish my father wouldn't try
to fix things anymore,
for everything he's mended
is more broken than before,
if my father finally fixes
every item on his list,
we'll be living in the garden,
for our house will not exist.

JACK PRELUTSKY

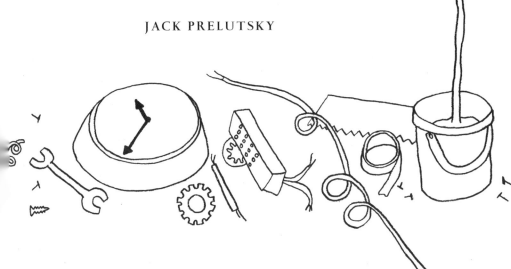

FRED

I haven't got a dad.
But I'm not sad.
I live with my mum.
My mum's got a boyfriend
– he's real good fun.
His name is Fred.
He drives a lorry.
The lorry's red.
He takes me with him:
we bomb down the road,
we go to a caff,
and then we unload.
He calls me his mate.
I think Fred's great.

NIGEL GRAY

THE SKATEBOARD

My daddy has bought me a skateboard;
    he tried it out first at the store.
And that is the reason why Mommy
    says Daddy can't walk anymore.

WILLARD R. ESPY

WALKING

Father's legs are very long.
He seldom walks for fun.
He mostly walks for getting there,
Which makes ME have to run.

AILEEN FISHER

IN DADDY'S ARMS

in daddy's arms i am tall
& close to the sun & warm
in daddy's arms

in daddy's arms
i can see over the fence out back
i can touch the bottom leaves of the big magnolia tree
in Cousin Sukie's yard
in daddy's arms

in my daddy's arms the moon is close
closer at night time when i can almost touch it
when it grins back at me from the wide twinkling skies

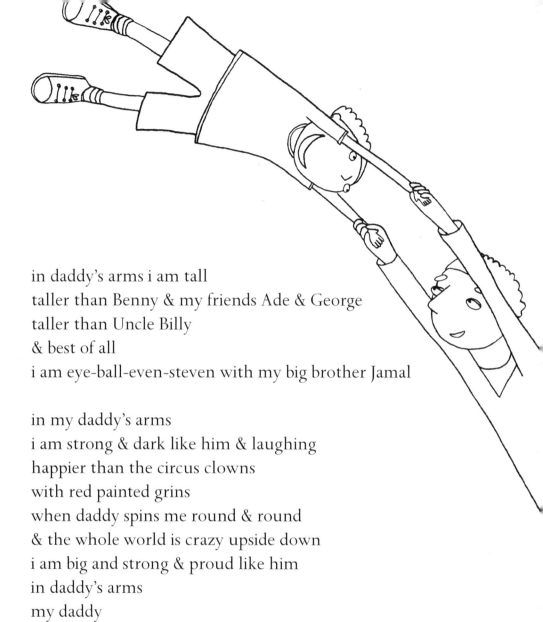

in daddy's arms i am tall
taller than Benny & my friends Ade & George
taller than Uncle Billy
& best of all
i am eye-ball-even-steven with my big brother Jamal

in my daddy's arms
i am strong & dark like him & laughing
happier than the circus clowns
with red painted grins
when daddy spins me round & round
& the whole world is crazy upside down
i am big and strong & proud like him
in daddy's arms
my daddy

FOLAMI ABIADE

THE TRICK

One night, when I couldn't sleep,
My Dad said
Think of the tomatoes in the greenhouse

And I did.
It wasn't the same as counting sheep
Or anything like that.

It was just not being in my room forever
On a hot bed
Restless, turning and turning,

But out there, with the patient gaze of moonlight
Blessing each ripe skin
And our old zinc watering-can with its sprinkler,

Shining through a clear glass pane
Which slowly clouded over into
Drowsy, comfortable darkness.

Till I woke and came downstairs to breakfast
Saying *Thank you, Dad,*
I thought of them. It did the trick.

JOHN MOLE

AUTOMOBILE MECHANICS

Sometimes
I help my dad
Work on our automobile.
We unscrew
The radiator cap
And let some water run—
Swish—from a hose
Into the tank.

And then we open up the hood
And feed in oil
From a can with a long spout.
And then we take a lot of rags
And clean all about.
We clean the top
And the doors
And the fenders and the wheels
And the windows and the floors . . .
And work hard
My dad
And I.

DOROTHY BARUCH

PEARLS

Dad gave me a string of pearls for my birthday.
They aren't real pearls but they look real.
They came nested in deep, deep blue velvet
    in a hinged box with a silvery lid.
His sister had some like them when she was my age.
She was thrilled.
He thought I'd really like them.
I said I did.

I love the box.

JEAN LITTLE

LIES

My father lied for me
when I refused to go to school
no special reason
except it was Monday
and raining
I blamed a headache but
he knew it wasn't true

He brought me aspirins
in a glass of water
said "your mother would
have known what to do"
then I heard him phone
"there's been a spot of
trouble in the past

I'd like to let you know
today he's genuinely ill"
teatime he asked me
"how are you now son?"
my head was thumping from
watching videos all day
"fine" I said "just fine"

IRENE RAWNSLEY

MY DAD

I love to watch my dad
when he's cutting his toenails.
My dad does not mind
if he has an audience.
He is like a medical T.V. show
during a tricky operation.
He says, "First you trim the nail
leaving a strip of white at the top
before probing under the nail for crud."
The crud is all different colours
because it is fluff from his socks.
He cannot understand people
who think that's all there is
to cutting your nails.
Neither can I.
Next he wedges a tiny pair of silver scissors
into the corner and takes another scissors
and goes clip, clip, clip.
That's for ingrown toenails.
To polish things off,
he scrapes the sides of his nail
with a little file just in case.
I would like to be as skilled
as my dad at cutting toenails
in the years to come.

JULIE O'CALLAGHAN

FLOWERS

My stepfather brought me flowers today.
For my first solo—my first bouquet,
yellow and peach and purple and red,
"Daughter, you sang like an angel," he said.
My stepfather brought me flowers, and I
pretended there wasn't a tear in his eye,
flowers and happiness tied with a bow,
because I had just sung my first solo.

ELOISE GREENFIELD

TICKLE TICKLE

me papa tickle me feet
he call it "finger treat"
me scream and run each time he come
me papa tickle me feet

he tickle me tummy, me chest, me arm
his fingers fly so wild
he say, "Come here, little man.
You my ticklin' chile."

me papa say he love me
me papa look so proud
he say, "Sonny, what a joy
to see you laugh out loud."

he tickle me ribs, me neck, me back
his fingers grow longer each day
me twist and swing and laugh and kick
but he hold me anyway

me eyes, they water
me throat be sore
me weak, me dizzy
but me want more

he throw me high up in the air
and catch me from behind
me say, "Go higher!" and he say,
"Don't you know you're mine?"

me papa tickle me feet
he call it "finger treat"
me scream and run (but OH, WHAT FUN!)
when papa tickle me feet

DAKARI HRU

THE PANTOMIME

Regularly at Christmas-time
We're taken to the Pantomime;
We think it's childish, but we go
Because Papa enjoys it so.

GUY BOAS

Never stew your sister

BROTHER AND SISTER

"Sister, sister, go to bed,
Go and rest your weary head,"
Thus the prudent brother said.

"Do you want a battered hide
Or scratches to your face applied?"
Thus the sister calm replied.

"Sister! do not rouse my wrath,
I'd make you into mutton broth
As easily as kill a moth."

The sister raised her beaming eye,
And looked on him indignantly,
And sternly answered "Only try!"

Off to the cook he quickly ran,
"Dear cook, pray lend a frying pan
To me, as quickly as you can."

"And wherefore should I give it you?"
"The reason, cook, is plain to view,
I wish to make an Irish stew."

"What meat is in that stew to go?"
"My sister'll be the contents." "Oh!"
"Will you lend the pan, cook?" "NO!"

MORAL: **"Never stew your sister."**

LEWIS CARROLL

TRIOLET AGAINST SISTERS

Sisters are always drying their hair.
　　Locked into rooms, alone,
They pose at the mirror, shoulders bare,
Trying this way and that their hair,
Or fly importunate down the stair
　　To answer a telephone.
Sisters are always drying their hair,
　　Locked into rooms, alone.

PHYLLIS McGINLEY

TANTRUMS

When my sister starts to frown
I'm always on my guard

Yesterday she threw a tantrum
But it missed me by a yard.

ROGER McGOUGH

MY SISTER LAURA

My sister Laura's bigger than me
And lifts me up quite easily.
I can't lift her, I've tried and tried;
She must have something heavy inside.

SPIKE MILLIGAN

MY HALF

I share a room
with brother Bob.
We share a bunk bed, too.
Half the room belongs to me,
and half to you-know-who.
Of course it's fair to share a room,
but yet I have the feeling
that since I'm on the upper bunk
my half's just on the ceiling.

FLORENCE PARRY HEIDE
& ROXANNE HEIDE PIERCE

TWO IN BED

When my brother Tommy
Sleeps in bed with me,
He doubles up
And makes
himself
exactly
like
a
V
And 'cause the bed is not so wide,
A part of him is on my side.

A. B. ROSS

SKATING ON THIN LINO

Because there is no Ice Rink
Within fifty miles of our house,
My sister perfects her dance routines
In the Olympic Stadium of my bedroom.
Wearing a soft expression
And two big, yellow dusters on her feet,
She explodes out of cupboards
To an avalanche of music
And whirls about the polished lino
in a blur of double axels and triple salchows.
For her free-style doubles
She hurls this pillow called Torvill
From here to breakfast-time
While spinning like a hippo
Round and round my bed.
Imagine waking up to that each morning;
Small wonder my hands shake
And I'm off my cornflakes.
Last Thursday she even made me
Stand up on my bed
And hold up cards marked "Six"
While she gave victory salutes
In the direction of the gerbil's cage.
To be honest,
Despite her endless dedication
And her hours of practice
I don't think she has a hope
Of lifting the world title.

But who cares?
She may not get the gold
But I'll bet there isn't another skater alive
With wall-to-wall mirror
On her bedroom floor.

GARETH OWEN

TO P.J.
(2 YRS OLD WHO SED WRITE A POEM
FOR ME IN PORTLAND, OREGON)

if i cud ever write a
poem as beautiful as u
little 2/yr/old/brotha,
i wud laugh, jump, leap
up and touch the stars
cuz u be the poem i try for
each time i pick up a pen and paper.
u. and Morani and Mungu
be our blue/blk/stars that
will shine on our lives and
make us finally BE.
if i cud ever write a poem as beautiful
as u, little 2/yr/old/brotha,
poetry wud go out of bizness.

SONIA SANCHEZ

MY BROTHER

My brother's worth about two cents,
As far as I can see.
I simply cannot understand
Why they would want a "he."

He spends a good part of his day
Asleep inside the crib,
And when he eats, he has to wear
A stupid baby bib.

He cannot walk and cannot talk
And cannot throw a ball.
In fact, he can't do anything—
He's just no fun at all.

It would have been more sensible,
As far as I can see,
Instead of getting one like him
To get one just like me.

MARCI RIDLON

MY BROTHER'S ON THE FLOOR ROARING

My brother's on the floor roaring
my brother's on the floor roaring
why is my brother on the floor roaring?
My brother is on the floor roaring
because he's supposed to finish his beans
before he has his pudding.

But he doesn't want to finish his beans
before he has his pudding

he says he wants his pudding
NOW.

But they won't let him

so now my brother is . . . on the floor roaring.

They're saying
I give you one more chance to finish those beans
or you don't go to Tony's
but he's not listening because . . .
he's on the floor roaring.

He's getting told off
I'm not
I've eaten my beans.

Do you know what I'm doing now?
I'm eating my pudding
and . . . he's on the floor roaring.

If he wasn't . . . on the floor roaring
he'd see me eating my pudding
and if he looked really close
he might see a little tiny smile
just at the corner of my mouth.
But he's not looking . . .
he's on the floor roaring.

The pudding is OK
it's not wonderful
not wonderful enough
to be sitting on the floor and roaring about
unless you're my brother.

MICHAEL ROSEN

I WISH I WAS

I wish I was
An only child
No brothers or sisters
To drive me wild

    I wish I had
    An older brother
    And a sister
    And another

I hate it when
We have a fight
I'm always wrong
They're always right

    I hate it when
    There's no one there
    To play with me
    To laugh, to share

TONY BRADMAN

I HAVE NONE

Robert has a baby sister
Kay has a baby sister
Kimani and Ayo both have
baby brothers
Janice and Sita have big brothers
and Justin's got a big sister.

All the kids have brothers and sisters
but I have none.

AFUA COOPER

AARON

Aaron

My Older Brother
Once Told Me He
Was The Ruler Of   This Hedge
Last
Year I Had To Have Permission
To Pick Wild Violets   For Mom

This   Morning   Aaron
                              Sits
                             In A
                           School
And I Am   The New Boss
Of Hedge Trees
And Mole Holes
And Violets   And   Black Bugs
                            Under
                            Green
                            Moss

ARNOLD ADOFF

I CAN UNTANGLE LINES

so
they think my brother's cute
just because he wears a pink singlet
and board shorts
that look like a mouldy fruit salad

and blonde hair that sticks up
and long brown legs
and goes to high school

I've got old footy shorts
a new fishing rod
a red plastic bucket
with cockles
and a rag
and a knife in it

and I can untangle lines
all by myself

JO CHESHER

SISTERS

She calls me tofu
because I am so soft,
easily falling apart.

I wish I were tough
and full of fire, like ginger—
like her.

JANET S. WONG

LITTLE SISTER

little sister
holds on tight.
My hands hurt
from all that squeezing,
but I don't mind.
She thinks no one will bother her
when I'm around,
and they won't
if I can help it.
And even when I can't,
I try
'cause she believes in me.

NIKKI GRIMES

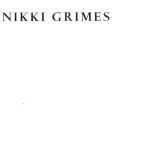

TRICKS

Nearly every morning
my brother would lie in bed,
lift his hands up in the air
full stretch
then close his hands around an invisible bar.
"Ah, my magic bar," he'd say.
Then he'd heave on the bar,
pull himself up,
until he was sitting up in bed.

Then he'd get up.
I said,
"You haven't got a magic bar above your bed."
"I have," he said.
"You haven't," I said.
"Don't believe me then," he said.
"I won't – don't worry," I said.
"It doesn't make any difference to me
if you do or you don't," he said,
and went out of the room.

"Magic bar!" I said.
"Mad. He hasn't got a magic bar."
I made sure he'd gone downstairs,
then I walked over to his bed
and waved my hand about in the air
above his pillow.
"I knew it," I said to myself.
"Didn't fool me for a moment."

MICHAEL ROSEN

LITTLE BROTHER'S SECRET

When my birthday was coming
Little Brother had a secret
He kept it for days and days
And just hummed a little tune when I asked him.
But one night it rained
And I woke up and heard him crying.
Then he told me
"I planted two lumps of sugar in your garden
Because you love it so frightfully
I thought there would be a whole sugar tree for
    your birthday
And now it will all be melted."
O, the darling!

KATHERINE MANSFIELD

LITTLE BROTHER

Listen, little brother,
this is **my** stuff.
So just leave it tidy
or I'll have to get tough.

Mind what you fiddle with
and don't be a pain,
or I'll never, ever, ever, *EVER*
talk to you again!

TONY MITTON

MY BROTHER

I used to think
how good it would be
if I was the onliest
kid in this house.
But when you went to camp,
I was the loneliest.

BOBBI KATZ

My other Granny

GRANDMA'S BONES

Grandma grew up
in the nineteen-forties
she can still do the jitterbug
a dance they used to do
to the music of Duke Ellington,
Benny Carter, Count Basie
and such

she can spin a yo-yo
much better than I
and sometimes she puts
two sticks called bones
between the knuckles
of one hand and goes

clack clack clackety
clackety clack
clackety clackety clackety
clack clack
uh clackety clack
uh clackety clack
clack clack clackety
clackety clack!

ELOISE GREENFIELD

THE OLDER THE VIOLIN
THE SWEETER THE TUNE

Me Granny old
Me Granny wise
stories shine like a moon
from inside she eyes.

Me Granny can dance
Me Granny can sing
but she can't play violin.

Yet she always saying,
"Dih older dih violin
de sweeter de tune."

Me Granny must be wiser
than the man inside the moon.

JOHN AGARD

GOODBYE GRANNY

Goodbye Granny
it's nearly time to fly
goodbye Granny
I am going in the sky.
I have my suitcase
and things.
You have packed
me everything
except the sunshine.
All our good times
are stored
up inside
more than enough
for any plane ride.
Goodbye Granny
things will be all right
goodbye Granny
I won't forget to write.
Goodbye Granny
bye! bye!
bye! bye!

PAULINE STEWART

GRANNY GRANNY PLEASE COMB MY HAIR

Granny Granny
please comb my hair
you always take your time
you always take such care

You put me to sit on a cushion
between your knees
you rub a little coconut oil
parting gentle as a breeze

Mummy Mummy
she's always in a hurry-hurry
rush
she pulls my hair
sometimes she tugs

But Granny
you have all the time in the world
and when you're finished
you always turn my head and say
"Now who's a nice girl."

GRACE NICHOLS

GRANDMOTHER

if i were to see
her shape from a mile away
i'd know so quickly
that it would be her.
the purple scarf
and the plastic
shopping bag.
if i felt
hands on my head
i'd know that those
were her hands
warm and damp
with the smell
of roots.
if i heard
a voice
coming from
a rock
i'd know
and her words
would flow inside me
like the light
of someone
stirring ashes
from a sleeping fire
at night.

RAY A. YOUNG BEAR

LINEAGE

My grandmothers were strong.
They followed plows and bent to toil.
They moved through fields sowing seed.
They touched earth and grain grew.
They were full of sturdiness and singing.
My grandmothers were strong.

My grandmothers are full of memories
Smelling of soap and onions and wet clay
With veins rolling roughly over quick hands
They have many clean words to say.
My grandmothers were strong.
Why am I not as they?

MARGARET WALKER

WHEN MY GRANDMOTHER DIED

When my grandmother died
I cried and cried
until I couldn't
open my eyes

She was the whole world
to me
big and round
and all full
of hugs

She was my favorite

When my grandmother died
I didn't want it
to be sunny no more
because nothing was funny
no more

She was my everything
my protector and friend
she didn't let nobody
pick on me
and always had
nice things to say
even when she didn't
feel good that day

When my grandmother died
I cried and cried

TONY MEDINA

GRANNY'S NINETY-TWO-YEAR-OLD LEGS

Granny's Ninety-Two-Year-Old Legs

Are Aching This October Morning   The Sun Is Bright   In The Pale
Blue
Sky
But She Says Her Shin Bones Have Been Hurting   Clear To   Winter

There Will Be   Falling
Weather By The Feel Of Her Legs   And   She Knows
That   Barometer   At   The   Weather   Station
Will   Follow   Right   Along   By   Evening
And There Will Be Cold And Rain Through
The Night

Granny's   Ninety-Two-Year-Old   Legs
Are
Almost
Always
Right

ARNOLD ADOFF

GLORY, GLORY . . .

Across Grandmother's knees
A kindly sun
Laid a yellow quilt.

RAYMOND R. PATTERSON

A SUITCASE OF SEAWEED

Across the ocean
from Korea
my grandmother,
my Halmoni,
has come—
her suitcase
sealed shut
with tape,
packed full
of sheets
of shiny black
seaweed
and stacks
of dried squid.
We break it open,
this old treasure
chest of hers,
holding
our noses
tight
as we release
its ripe
sea smell.

JANET S. WONG

MY OTHER GRANNY

My Granny is an Octopus
   At the bottom of the sea,
And when she comes to supper
   She brings her family.

She chooses a wild wet windy night
   When the world rolls blind
As a boulder in the night-sea surf,
   And her family troops behind.

The sea-smell enters with them
   As they sidle and slither and spill
With their huge eyes and their tiny eyes
   And a dripping ocean-chill.

Some of her cousins are lobsters
   Some floppy jelly fish –
What would you be if your family tree
   Grew out of such a dish?

Her brothers are crabs jointed and knobbed
  With little pinhead eyes,
Their pincers crack the biscuits
  And they bubble joyful cries.

Crayfish the size of ponies
  Creak as they sip their milk.
My father stares in horror
  At my mother's secret ilk.

They wave long whiplash antennae,
  They sizzle and they squirt –
We smile and waggle our fingers back
  Or grandma would be hurt.

"What's new, Ma?" my father asks,
  "Down in the marvellous deep?"
Her face swells up, her eyes bulge huge
  And she begins to weep.

She knots her sucker tentacles
    And gapes like a nestling bird,
And her eyes flash, changing stations,
    As she attempts a WORD –

Then out of her eyes there brim two drops
    That plop into her saucer –
And that is all she manages,
    And my Dad knows he can't force her.

And when they've gone, my ocean-folk,
    No man could prove they came –
For the sea-tears in her saucer
    And a man's tears are the same.

TED HUGHES

TIME TO DUST THE DAFFODILS

My gran's too old
to go out
in the cold garden
planting bulbs,
but she likes
spring flowers.

She has a box
of plastic daffodils
on sticks
that she hides away
in the winter.

When she notices
that spring is coming
she takes them out,
dusts each one
carefully,

then plants them
underneath her window.

Passers-by pause
to admire them.
"How lovely, Mrs Paradine!
Why do your daffodils
always bloom earlier
than mine?"

IRENE RAWNSLEY

MOUNTAIN MOON AND GOLD

Grandmother is getting slower and complains
that her heart clock is running late.
Grandfather slaps her on the bottom and laughs
that no matter how old
she has not even begun
to catch up mountain moon and gold.

PAULINE STEWART

Lucky to be little

BABIES

Babies are funny.
They don't speak a lot.
They can't drink from cups
Or sit on a pot.

They like to grip fingers.
They like milk from Mummies.
They like having raspberries
Blown on their tummies.

They like being cuddled
And kissed on the head.
But they don't say a lot,
They just dribble instead.

MICHELLE MAGORIAN

MUM IS HAVING A BABY!

Mum is having a baby!
   I'm shocked! I'm all at sea!
What's she want another one for:
   WHAT'S THE MATTER WITH ME!?

COLIN McNAUGHTON

LEAKY BABY

Our brand new baby's sprung a leak!
He's dripping like a spout.
We'd better send him back
Before the guarantee runs out.

KAYE UMANSKY

LITTLE SISTER

That's my little sister
Just five minutes old
Already seeking something
To bite and chew and hold,
That's my little sister
Already going bald
I can't just call her sister
So what will she be called?

I want to call her Carol
But all carols are hymns
I want to call her Jimmy
But I always visit gyms,
I want to call her spotty
But she may punch my nose
I will not call her Rosy
She don't look like a rose.

When I hear her crying
I want to call her *loud*
If she's the type for talking
I may call her a *crowd,*
If she's good at singing
I'll call her *nightingale*
If she keeps on grinning
She'll make the doctors wail.

The doctors called her beauty
But beauty is a horse
The nurses called her cutey
Being polite of course,
My Mummy and my Daddy
Just don't have an idea
We don't have a name ready
But we're so glad she's here.

BENJAMIN ZEPHANIAH

A WELCOME SONG FOR LAINI NZINGA

Born November 24, 1975

Hello, little Sister.
Coming through the rim of the world.
We are here! to meet you and to mold and to maintain you.
With excited eyes we see you.
With welcoming ears we hear the
clean sound of new language.
The language of Laini Nzinga.
We love and we receive you as our own.

GWENDOLYN BROOKS

BIRTH OF A BABY

January 16th, 1991,
Was all set to be an ordinary day,
But the ringing of the phone at seven-thirty
Changed that.
For nine months
My stepmum had carried a load,
Nine months of feeling
Like a beached whale.
That Wednesday,
Bethany Clare was born.
It was my dad on the phone,
Telling the good news,
"Mother and baby both fit and well."
That night I went to visit.
She was so small,
So delicate,
So harmless.
I held her;
She is beautiful,
My half sister.

GEMMA CHILVERS

BRILLIANT – LIKE ME

today I went with Mum
and Dad on the bus and
the train for our baby

it took us three hours
to travel all that way
but we knew she'd be
worth the long journey

our baby and me are
adopted, but we both
have freckly skin
and I laughed today
when I saw her – she
gave me a gummy grin

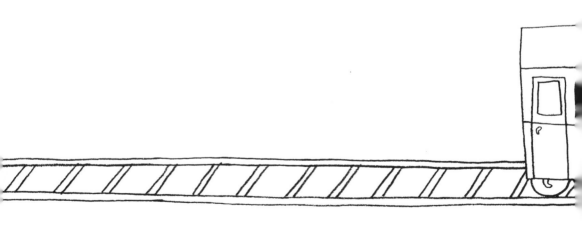

I laughed when I saw
her — looking just
like me, she's even got
a funny pointy chin

I'm glad Mum and Dad
chose our baby — I'm
glad they both chose me
it's going to be great
to have a little sister

I think she's brilliant
like me.

JOAN POULSON

NEW BABY

My baby brother makes so much noise
that the Rottweiler next door
phoned up to complain.

My baby brother makes so much noise
that all the big green frogs
came out the drains.

My baby brother makes so much noise
that the rats and the mice
wore headphones.

My baby brother makes so much noise
that I can't ask my mum a question,
so much noise that sometimes

I think of sitting the cat on top of him
in his pretty little cot with all his teddies.
But even the cat is terrified of his cries.

So I have devised a plan. A soundproof room.
A telephone to talk to my mum.
A small lift to receive food and toys.

Thing is, it will cost a fortune.
The other thing is, the frogs have gone.
It's not bad now. Not that I like him or anything.

JACKIE KAY

GRANDMA'S LULLABY

Close your eyes,
My precious love,
Grandma's little
Turtledove.

Go to sleep now,
Pretty kitty,
Grandma's little
Chickabiddy.

Stop your crying,
Cuddly cutie,
Grandma's little
Sweet patootie.

Issum, wissum,
Popsy wopsy,
Tootsie wootsie
Lollypopsie
Diddims
Huggle
Snuggle pup

And now, for Grandma's sake, hush up!

CHARLOTTE POMERANTZ

146

LIFE'S NOT BEEN THE SAME IN MY FAMILY

Life's not been the same in my family
since the day that the new baby came,
my parents completely ignore me,
they scarcely remember my name.

The baby gets all their attention,
"Oh, isn't she precious!" they croon,
they think that she looks like an angel,
I think she resembles a prune.

They're thrilled when she giggles or gurgles,
"She burped!" they exclaim with delight,
they don't even mind when she wakes us
with deafening screams in the night.

They seem to believe she's a treasure,
there's simply no way I agree,
I wish she'd stop being a baby
and start being older than me.

JACK PRELUTSKY

THE BABY OF THE FAMILY

Up on Daddy's shoulders
He is riding high –
The baby of the family,
A pleased, pork pie.
I'm tired and my feet are sore –
It seems all wrong.
He's lucky to be little
But it won't last long.

The baby of the family,
He grabs my toys
And when I grab them back he makes
A big, loud noise.
I mustn't hit him, so I chant
This short, sweet song:
"You're lucky to be little
But it won't last long."

Everybody looks at him
And thinks he's sweet,
Even when he bellows "No!"
And stamps his feet.
He won't be so amusing
When he's tall and strong.
It's lovely being little
But it won't last long.

WENDY COPE

LITTLE

I am the sister of him
And he is my brother.
He is too little for us
To talk to each other.

So every morning I show him
My doll and my book;
But every morning he still is
Too little to look.

DOROTHY ALDIS

Just like Grandpa

GRANDPA MILKING COWS

I'm off to the paddock,
running barefoot in the dew
with my Grandpa.

Grandpa pulling on the udders
fills his pail
with foaming milk.

Sipping warm milk,
I get a white mustache
just like Grandpa's.

MONICA GUNNING

BEDMOBILE

I hear my grandad on the stair
He's counting, One Two Three
Bringing a rosy apple plucked
From my special climbing tree.
He brings the garden in with him
The flowers and the air
And there are twigs and petals
Tangled in his hair.
And as I eat my apple
He sits down next to me
Turning an imaginary wheel
"Where to today?" says he.
And we drive our deluxe Bedmobile
To school along the heath
With the apple dribbling sweetness
Clenched between my teeth.

GARETH OWEN

SHED IN SPACE

My Grandad Lewis
On my mother's side
Had two ambitions.
One was to take first prize
For shallots at the village show
And the second
Was to be a space commander.
Every Tuesday
After I'd got their messages,
He'd lead me with a wink
To his garden shed
And there, amongst the linseed
And the sacks of peat and horse manure
He'd light his pipe
And settle in his deck chair.
His old eyes on the blue and distant
That no one else could see,
He'd ask,
"Are we A–OK for lift off?"
Gripping the handles of the lawn mower
I'd reply:
"A–OK."
And then
Facing the workbench,
In front of shelves of paint and creosote
And racks of glistening chisels
He'd talk to Mission Control.

"Five-Four-Three-Two-One-Zero —
We have lift off.
This is Grandad Lewis talking,
Do you read me?
Britain's first space shed
Is rising majestically into orbit
From its launch pad
In the allotments
In Lakey Lane."

And so we'd fly,
Through timeless afternoons
Till tea time came,
Amongst the planets
And mysterious suns,
While the world
Receded like a dream:
Grandad never won
That prize for shallots,
But as the captain
Of an intergalactic shed
There was no one to touch him.

GARETH OWEN

GRANDAD'S SHED

Grandad's shed is a secret place.
I love to go in there,
And when I say, "Please, Grandad, please!"
He finds the key, unlocks the door,
And we step inside.

There's watering cans and a lawnmower,
Forks and flowerpots too.
A spade, a rake, a trowel,
Sharp saws for cutting through.

There's sticks and bags and paint tins,
Seed packets, balls of string,
A stepladder, a box of tools,
All sorts of curious things.

When we've finished looking,
And closed the door and turned the key,
What does my Grandad do?

He swings me high, then sits me down,
Snug in his green wheelbarrow.
"Hold tight!" he says,
And off we go,
The two of us together.

MARGARET MAYO

MY GRAMP

My gramp has got a medal.
On the front there is a runner.
On the back it says:
Senior Boys 100 Yards
First William Green.
I asked him about it,
but before he could reply
Gran said, "Don't listen to his tales.
The only running he ever did
was after the girls."
Gramp gave a chuckle
and went out the back
to get the tea.
As he shuffled down the passage
with his back bent,
I tried to imagine him,
legs flying, chest out,
breasting the tape.
But I couldn't.

JOHN FOSTER

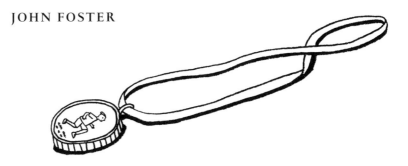

GRANDPA

Grandpa's hands are as rough as garden sacks
And as warm as pockets.
His skin is crushed paper round his eyes
Wrapping up their secrets.

BERLIE DOHERTY

WHEN I GROW UP

I want to be an artist, Grandpa—
write and paint, dance and sing.

> Be accountant.
> Be lawyer.
> Make good living,
> buy good food.
> Back in China,
> in the old days,
> everybody
> so, so poor.
> Eat one chicken,
> work all year.

Grandpa, things are different
here.

JANET S. WONG

GRANDAD'S LOST HIS GLASSES

Grandad's lost his glasses
He thinks they're by his bed
We're far too mean to tell him
That they're perched upon his head.

LINDSAY MacRAE

Remembering

TOAST

I remember my Dad he was the best Dad
anyone could have
When my sister and I were young
We had such fun.
When my Mum went out for a drink,
which she did most nights,
My Dad would get out the bread
and toast it on the fire for us.
We thought this was a great treat,
with cheese on top
We would sit and he would tell us stories
of when he was a lad.
I have tasted toast which other people have made
But it wasn't as good as my Dad's.

MAUREEN NATT

REMEMBERING

remembering
Grandma filling up this porch
with laughing
and stories about when
Mama was a little girl
and Grandma would hug me
and say
I was her very special own granddaughter.
But now she's gone.
I miss her—

NIKKI GRIMES

GOING THROUGH THE OLD PHOTOS

Who's that?
That's your Auntie Mabel
and that's me
under the table.

Who's that?
That's Uncle Billy.
Who's that?
Me being silly.

Who's that
licking a lolly?
I'm not sure
but I think it's Polly.

Who's that
behind the tree?
I don't know,
I can't see.
Could be you.
Could be me.

Who's that?
Baby Joe.
Who's that?
I don't know.

Who's that standing
on his head?
Turn it round.
It's Uncle Ted.

MICHAEL ROSEN

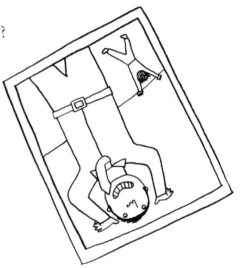

FAMILY PHOTO

I can't believe it's my Dad
Standing there
His hair all golden
His bottom bare
Two little dimples in his face

When now, all fat and bald
With straggly eyebrows
Which he just won't cut,
He's more like something
From another race.

JOHN KITCHING

A FAMILY PHOTO

This is my dad,
That's my step-mum, Irene,
And this is the baby, Annie.
That's their dog, Dozer,
He's so funny,
He always sits under the table.

No, I'm not in that picture.

LYNETTE CRAIG

ODE TO FAMILY PHOTOGRAPHS

This is the pond, and these are my feet.
This is the rooster, and this is more of my feet.

Mamá was never good at pictures.

This is a statue of a famous general who lost an arm,
And this is me with my head cut off.

This is a trash can chained to a gate,
This is my father with his eyes half-closed.

This is a photograph of my sister
And a giraffe looking over her shoulder.

This is our car's front bumper.
This is a bird with a pretzel in its beak.
This is my brother Pedro standing on one leg on a rock,
With a smear of chocolate on his face.

Mamá sneezed when she looked
Behind the camera: the snapshots are blurry,
The angles dizzy as a spin on a merry-go-round.

But we had fun when Mamá picked up the camera.
How can I tell?
Each of us laughing hard.
Can you see? I have candy in my mouth.

GARY SOTO

THE PICTURE

There's a picture that my dad's got,
    He keeps it by his bed,
Of him when he was little,
    With my grandpa, who's dead.

They're standing close together,
    On a day out at the fair;
Grandpa's got his arm round Dad.
    No one else is there.

Both of them are smiling,
    And looking straight ahead;
My dad with his father,
    With my grandpa, who's dead.

I never knew my grandpa,
    And he never knew of me,
But even though we didn't meet
    We're still family.

Dad looks just like Grandpa,
    And I'm like Dad, Mum said;
Which means I look like Grandpa,
    My grandpa, who's dead.

They're happy in that picture,
    On a day out at the fair;
And I know it's strange to say it,
    But I wish that I'd been there.

There before the camera,
    Looking straight ahead,
With my dad when he was little,
    And my grandpa, who's dead.

TONY BRADMAN

MAMA

Mama was funny
was full of jokes
was pretty
dark brown-skinned
laughter
was hard hugs
and kisses
a mad mama
sometimes
but always
always
was love

ELOISE GREENFIELD

MY WHOLE FAMILY

I can
remember what
things were like before she
got sick: my whole family climbed
into

the big
hammock on the
moondappled beach, wove
ourselves together, and swayed
as one.

SONYA SONES

CINEMA

Special Saturday
Half-price matinée,
Grandma's holiday.

She likes to tell it out to us
Spell it out to us —
How she loved to go
To a show
Long ago.

And all about
The sweet-scented
Faded
Gold-painted
Fusty
Dusty
Screen dream
Massive screen . . . .
Rainbow dream . . . .

"Fifty years ago this was a palace! (said my grandmother)
A glass and chromium
Theatre Organolean
Would rise
To the skies
In a flickering
Gilt glittering
Criss-crossing of coloured light spots –
And Boom . . . . !
Through the Gloom . . . . (said my grandmother)"

I wish *I* could have seen it when
It was all plush and gold;
Now it just looks old –
But it must have been a palace then,
Just as grandma told.

MARIAN LINES

FOLDING SHEETS

They must be clean.
There ought to be two of you
to talk as you work, your
eyes and hands meeting.
They can be crisp, a little rough
and fragrant from the line;
or hot from the dryer
as from the oven. A silver
grey kitten with amber
eyes to dart among
the sheets and wrestle and leap out
helps. But mostly pleasure
lies in the clean linen
slapping into shape.
Whenever I fold a fitted sheet
making the moves that are like
closing doors, I feel my mother.
The smell of clean laundry is hers.

MARGE PIERCEY

GROWN-UP BLUES

Mother used to come when I was sick,
give me a thermometer to check my fever,
make me swallow orange aspirins
(the ones for kids)
and tuck me in bed.

Dad used to come when I was sick,
feel my forehead,
and ask if my chest hurt,
and tell me to lie down when I already was.

Nobody comes now when I'm sick.
I have to feel my own forehead,
take my own temperature,
and swallow two white aspirins
(the ones for adults).

TERRY KEE

MISSING MAMA

last year when Mama died
I went to my room to hide
from the hurt
I closed my door
wasn't going to come out
no more, never
but my uncle he said
you going to get past
this pain
      you going to
push on past this pain
and one of these days
you going to feel like
yourself again
I don't miss a day
remembering Mama
sometimes I cry
but mostly
I think about
the good things
now

ELOISE GREENFIELD

TEASED

Sometimes
when I'm teased
I don't cry,
I go away.
When I come back
my brother and his friends
are doing something else.
I remember.
They forget.

RICHARD J. MARGOLIS

I KEEP A PHOTO OF MY GRANDMOTHER

I keep a photo of my Grandmother.
I have never seen my Grandmother.
I keep a photo of her
in my rose box.
My Grandmother
sitting on a chair
in the garden.

SAU YEE KAN

Mother doesn't want a dog

CAT KISSES

Sandpaper kisses
on a cheek or a chin—
that is the way
for a day to begin!

Sandpaper kisses—
a cuddle, a purr.
I have an alarm clock
that's covered with fur.

BOBBI KATZ

MY DOG

My dog is such a gentle soul,
Although he's big it's true.
He brings the paper in his mouth,
He brings the postman too.

MAX FATCHEN

ODE TO A GOLDFISH

O
Wet
Pet!

GYLES BRANDRETH

MY GERBIL

My gerbil doesn't bite
But if you poke him
then he might . . .

RIK MARTIN

MOTHER DOESN'T WANT A DOG

Mother doesn't want a dog.
Mother says they smell,
And never sit when you say sit,
Or even when you yell.
And when you come home late at night
And there is ice and snow,
You have to go back out because
The dumb dog has to go.

Mother doesn't want a dog.
Mother says they shed,
And always let the strangers in
And bark at friends instead,
And do disgraceful things on rugs,
And track mud on the floor,
And flop upon your bed at night
And snore their doggy snore.

Mother doesn't want a dog.
She's making a mistake.
Because, more than a dog, I think
She will not want this snake.

JUDITH VIORST

OUR HAMSTER'S LIFE

Our hamster's life:
there's not much
to it,
not much
to it.

He presses his pink nose
to the door of his cage
and decides for the fifty-six
millionth time
that he can't get
through it.

Our hamster's life;
there's not much
to it,
not much
to it.

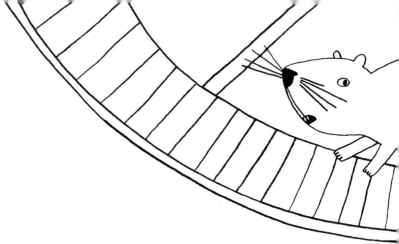

It's about the most boring
life in the world,
if he only
knew it.
He sleeps and he drinks and he eats.
He eats and he drinks and he sleeps.

He slinks and he dreeps.
He eats.

This process
he repeats.

Our hamster's life:
there's not much
to it,
not much
to it.

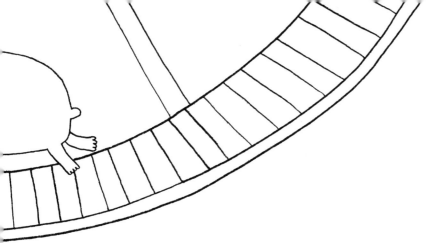

You'd think it would drive him bonkers,
going round and round on his wheel.
It's certainly driving me bonkers,

watching him
do it.

But he may be thinking:
"That boy's life,
there's not much
to it,
not much
to it:

watching a hamster go round on a wheel.
It's driving me bonkers if he only knew it,

watching him
watching me
do it."

KIT WRIGHT

GREEDY DOG

This dog will eat anything.

Apple cores and bacon fat,
Milk you poured out for the cat.
He likes the string that ties the roast
And relishes hot buttered toast.
Hide your chocolates! He's a thief,
He'll even eat your handkerchief.
And if you don't like sudden shocks,
Carefully conceal your socks.
Leave some soup without a lid
And you'll wish you never did.
When you think he must be full,
You find him gobbling bits of wool,
Orange peel or paper bags,
Dusters and old cleaning rags.

This dog will eat anything,
Except for mushrooms and cucumber.

Now what is wrong with those, I wonder.

JAMES HURLEY

HIS DOG

My brother shuffles through the door
carrying little Sandy in his arms.
His tears make Sandy's fur wet.
When I try to pet her head,
he pulls away. "Don't," he says.
"She's dead."
Then I pet my brother's head.
She was his dog.

RICHARD J. MARGOLIS

MY CAT

My cat
got fatter
and fatter.
I didn't know
what was the matter.
Then,
know what she did?
She went into the cupboard
and hid.

She was fat when she went in,
but she came out
thin.
I had a peep.
Know what I saw?
Little kittens
all in a heap
$-1-2-3-4.$

My cat's great.

NIGEL GRAY

AMBER

I think that the tortoise-shell cat
Who lives with my aunt
Is a bewitched thing:
By no means, wholly, only, cat.
She's a shape-shifter, a body-changer,
Who in turn has been
Phoenix, mermaid, hippogriff.
Through feather and skin and scale
Her slit green eyes have seen
Glass mountains, emerald caves,
And the outer rims of space.
For this stately, crazy puss
Now roams for hours
On the soft South Downs,
In sheep's form, owl's plumes,
Under snail's shell, moth's wings.
My aunt calls her back
With a clack of her scissors.
Then quickly in cat's skin,
Amber runs home
To play with string, purr with fire,
If they're alone.
Crouched in anger and fear,
She hides when I'm there.
Aunt says she hates strangers.

SHIRLEY TOULSON

THERE'S A DOG

There's a dog in a spaceship orbiting Mars.
There's a dog with its paw on the wheel of a car.
There's a dog born under a lucky star.
There's a dog.

There's a dog fast asleep in the bed of the Queen.
There's a dog autographing its name with a pen.
There's a dog in the sea in a submarine.
There's a dog.

There's a dog that doesn't eat socks and shoes.
There's a dog that hasn't got nothing to lose.
There's a dog that doesn't how-ow-owl the blues.
There's a dog.

There's a dog reading poetry under a lamp.
There's a dog's dog face on a first class stamp.
There's a dog out jogging despite its limp.
There's a dog.

There's a dog in the kitchen cooking a meal.
There's a dog with wings at God's right heel.
There's a dog hang-gliding in a Force 10 gale.
There's a dog.

There's a dog that doesn't chew table legs.
There's a dog that never whines and begs.
There's a dog that hasn't grown too big.
There's a dog.

There's a dog in goal at the FA Cup.
There's a dog teaching French to a newborn pup.
There's a dog in the City on the up-and-up.
There's a dog.

There's a dog in the charts at Number One.
There's a dog in charge at Number Ten.
There's a dog playing chance on number nine.
There's a dog.

There's a dog that doesn't bite small boys.
There's a dog that doesn't swallow toys.
There's a dog that doesn't bark at the slightest noise.
There's a dog.

There's a dog. There's a dog.
There's a dog. There's a dog.
There's a dog that DOESN'T LIVE WITH US.

CAROL ANN DUFFY

THANK YOU, DAD, FOR EVERYTHING

Thank you for laying the carpet, Dad,
Thank you for showing us how,
But what is that lump in the middle, Dad?
And why is it saying mia-ow?

DOUG MACLEOD

Tea with Aunty Mabel

TEA WITH AUNTY MABEL

If you ever go to tea with my Aunty Mabel,
Never put your elbows on the dining-room table,
Always wipe your shoes if you've been in the garden,
Don't ever burp. If you do, say pardon.
Don't put your feet on the new settee,
If she offers you a sugar lump, don't take three.
Don't dunk your biscuits, don't make crumbs,
Don't bite nails and don't suck thumbs.
Don't rock the budgie, don't tease the peke,
Speak when you're spoken to or else don't speak.
Do as you're told and if you're not able,
Don't go to tea with my Aunty Mabel.

JEANNE WILLIS

AUNT LOUISA

When Aunt Louisa lit the gas
   She had the queerest feeling.
Instead of leaving by the door
   She vanished through the ceiling.

MAX FATCHEN

THE AUNTIE WITH A KISS LIKE
A HEAT-SEEKING MISSILE

Auntie Enid loves to kiss
Seldom does she ever miss.

LINDSAY MacRAE

SAUCE

Aunt Ruth came from England
and guess all that we got —
a jar of English mustard
which she said was very hot.

"That yellow thing no pepper!"
remarked my aunty Dot.
"England famous for it strawberry
but for pepper it is not!"

Before we could prevent her
Aunt D dip in she big spoon.
It hot! it hot! so till
it nearly send her to the moon.

Now aunty Dot eats quietly
she scarcely speaks a word
she no touch the jar of mustard
since it deaden she taste-bud.

PAULINE STEWART

COUSIN JANICE WITH THE BIG VOICE

When my cousin Janice
Opens her mouth to speak
A storm kindles behind her teeth
And a gale pours out.
This is a voice used
To holding conversations
With cows and sheep and dogs
Across mountains and valleys
But here across the tablecloth
In our small flat
When she asks for the sugar
The teacups tremble
And a tidal wave foments
In the eddies of the cherry trifle.

GARETH OWEN

UNCLE

Uncle was Gran's brother,
came to stay when she died,
kept to his room at the top of the stairs
but on Sundays he polished shoes.

Uncle was expert, a real shoe sheriff.
Each Size 10 had a price on its head
till he rounded it up with the rest.
He'd lasso Mum's boots and whistle
till plimsolls came running.
He knew, of course, where I threw mine,
when one was missing, he'd corner the dog,
then search through his bed till he found it.

The shoes submitted instantly.
They waited, trembling in line,
while one by one Uncle slapped on polish,
cleaned off the week's wear and tear
then buffed them to a shine.

He'd brighten the shabbiest pair,
the ones that had skulked for months
in a cupboard beneath the stairs.
He'd untangle loops and knots
then leave the shoes in rows
till, like some general inspecting troops,
I'd signal which ones went back
for a second go.

I took on his job when he died,
cleaned shoes for money.
I'd rub away like Aladdin and think
how my efforts might free Uncle's ghost.
I knew how much he'd be missing that mix
of polish and Sunday roast.

BRIAN MOSES

WHEN I WAS YOUR AGE

My uncle said, "How do you get to school?"
I said, "By bus," and my uncle smiled.
"When I was your age," my uncle said,
"I walked it *barefoot—seven miles*."

My uncle said, "How much weight can you tote?"
I said, "One bag of grain." My uncle laughed.
"When I was your age," my uncle said,
"I could drive a wagon—and lift a *calf*."

My uncle said, "How many fights have you had?"
I said, "Two—and both times I got whipped."
"When I was your age," my uncle said,
"I fought every day—and was *never* licked."

My uncle said, "How old are you?"
I said, "Nine and a half," and then
My uncle puffed out his chest and said,
"When I was your age . . . I was *ten*."

SHEL SILVERSTEIN

SAID UNCLE

"There are people," said Uncle,
"Who bumble like bees.
There are people," said Uncle,
"With back to front knees.
There are people," said Uncle,
"Who breathe through one ear."
"There are people," said Auntie,
"Who shouldn't drink beer."

RICHARD EDWARDS

MY SNEAKY COUSIN

She put in her clothes,
Then thought she'd get
A free bath here
At the launderette.
So round she goes now,
Flippity-flappy,
Lookin' clean—
But not too happy.

SHEL SILVERSTEIN

FINDING OUT ABOUT THE FAMILY

It was really rather scary
When my dear old Auntie Mary
Started going very hairy
When the moon was full and bright,
And went outside on the prowl
With a loud and eerie howl
Like a wild wolf on a hilltop
In the middle of the night.

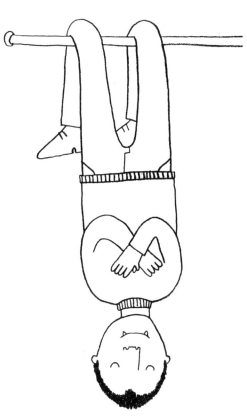

It was really rather odd
When I found my Uncle Tod
Dangling from a wooden rod
Where a curtain usually hangs,
He was upside down, in black,
With his hair slicked thinly back
And the firelight flickering fiercely
On the sharp tips of his fangs.

It was most bizarre of all
When my little brother Paul
Disappeared into the wall
In a puff of purple smoke,
Then my sister waved her wand,
And now I'm living in this pond
Eating flies and feeling slimy . . .
Ribbit ribbit, croak croak croak.

RICHARD EDWARDS

MADAM'S CHRISTMAS

I forgot to send
A card to Jennie—
But the truth about cousins is
There's too many.

I also forgot
My Uncle Joe
But I believe I'll let
That old rascal go.

I done bought
Four boxes now
I can't afford
No more, no how.

So Merry Xmas,
Everybody!
Cards or no cards
Here's HOWDY!

LANGSTON HUGHES

MANNERS

I have an uncle I don't like,
    An aunt I cannot bear:
She chucks me underneath the chin,
    He ruffles up my hair.

Another uncle I adore,
    Another aunty, too:
She shakes me kindly by the hand,
    He says, "How do you do?"

MARIANA GRISWOLD VAN RENSSELAER

FAMILY ALBUM

I wish I liked Aunt Leonora
When she draws in her breath with a hiss
And with fingers of ice and a grip like a vice
She gives me a walloping kiss.

I wish I loved Uncle Nathaniel
(The one with the teeth and the snore).
He's really a pain when he tells me *again*
About what he did in the War.

I really don't care for Aunt Millie,
Her bangles and brooches and beads,
Or the gun that she shoots or those ex-army boots
Or the terrible dogs that she breeds.

I simply can't stand Uncle Albert.
Quite frankly, he fills me with dread
When he gives us a tune with a knife, fork and spoon.
(I don't think he's right in the head.)

I wish I loved Hetty and Harry
(Aunt Hilary's horrible twins)
As they lie in their cots giving off lots and lots
Of gurgles and gargles and grins.

As for nieces or nephews or cousins
There seems nothing else one can do
Except sit in a chair and exchange a cold stare
As if we came out of a zoo.

Though they say blood is thicker than water,
I'm not at all certain it's so.
If you think it's the case, kindly write to this space.
It's something I'm anxious to know.

If we only could choose our relations
How happy, I'm certain, we'd be!
And just one thing more: I am perfectly sure
Mine all feel the same about me.

CHARLES CAUSLEY

Index of poets

Index of first lines

216

Acknowledgments

The publisher would like to thank the copyright holders for permission to reproduce the following copyright material:

Folami Abiade: "In Daddy's Arms" from *In My Daddy's Arms I Am Tall*, Lee & Low Books, 1997. Permission arranged with Lee & Low Books, Inc., New York, NY 10016. **Arnold Adoff**: "Aaron", "Granny's Ninety-Two-Year-Old Legs" and "I Am The Youngest" from *In for Winter, Out for Spring* by Arnold Adoff, copyright © 1991 by Arnold Adoff, reprinted by permission of Harcourt, Inc. **John Agard**: "Ask Mummy, Ask Daddy" from *I Din Do Nuttin* by John Agard, published by Bodley Head and "The Older the Violin the Sweeter the Tune" from *Say it Again Granny* by John Agard, published by Bodley Head. Used by permission of The Random House Group Limited. **Allan Ahlberg**: "Emma Hackett's Newsbook" from *Please Mrs Butler* by Allan Ahlberg (Kestrel, 1983). Copyright © Allan Ahlberg, 1983. Reproduced by permission of Penguin Books Ltd. **Dorothy Aldis**: "Everybody Says" from *Here, There and Everywhere* by Dorothy Aldis, copyright © 1927, 1928, copyright renewed © 1955, 1956 by Dorothy Aldis and "Little" from *Everything and Anything* by Dorothy Aldis, copyright © 1925–1927, renewed 1953, © 1954, 1955 by Dorothy Aldis. Used by permission of G.P. Putnam's Sons, an imprint of Penguin Putnam Books for Young Readers, a division of Penguin Putnam Inc. All rights reserved. **James Berry**: "Mum Dad and Me" from *When I Dance: Poems by James Berry*, Hamish Hamilton Children's Books, 1988. Reproduced by permission of PFD on behalf of James Berry. **Tony Bradman**: "I Wish I Was" excerpted from "I Wish" by Tony Bradman. Reproduced by permission of The Agency (London) Ltd. Copyright © Tony Bradman 1989. First published in *All Together Now*, Viking. All rights reserved and enquiries to The Agency (London) Ltd, 24 Pottery Lane, London W11 4LZ fax: 020 7727 9037. "The Picture" from *All Together Now*, Viking Books, 1989. Copyright © Tony Bradman 1989. Reproduced by permission of the author c/o Rogers, Coleridge & White Ltd., 20 Powis Mews, London W11 1JN. **Gyles Brandreth**: "Ode to a Goldfish" by Gyles Brandreth from *Pet Poems*, ed. Robert Fisher, Faber and Faber 1989. Reproduced by permission of the author. **Gwendolyn Brooks**: "A Welcome Song for Laini Nzinga" from *To Disembark*. Reprinted by permission of The Estate of Gwendolyn Brooks. **Charles Causley**: David Higham Associates for "Family Album" from *Collected Poems for Children* by Charles Causley, Macmillan. **Jo Chesher**: "I Can Untangle Lines" by Jo Chesher from *Rattling in the Wind: Australian Poems for Children*, selected by Jill Heylen and Celia Jellett, Adelaide: Omnibus Books, 1987. Reprinted by permission of the author. **Gemma Chilvers**: the author for "Birth of a Baby", copyright © Gemma Chilvers, from *Them and Us*, compiled by Jennifer Curry, Bodley Head, 1993. **Marchette Chute**: "School Concert" from *Rhymes About Us* by Marchette Chute, copyright © 1974 by E.P. Dutton. Reprinted by permission of Elizabeth Hauser. **Lucille Clifton**: "My Natural Mama". Copyright © 1988 by Lucille Clifton. First appeared in *Poems for Mothers*, published by Holiday House. Reprinted by permission of Curtis Brown, Ltd. **John Coldwell**: the author for "Mum Doesn't Live with Us Any More" from *All in the Family*, Oxford University Press, 1993. **Afua Cooper**: the author for "I Have None" from *Red Caterpillar on College Street* by Afua Cooper (Sister Vision Press, Toronto, 1989). **Wendy Cope**: "The Baby of the Family" reprinted with the author's permission. Copyright © Wendy Cope 1990. **Lynette Craig**: the author for "A Family Photo" by Lynette Craig from *All in the*

Family, Oxford University Press, 1993. **Peter Dixon**: the author for "My Daddy Dances Tapstep" from *Peter Dixon's Grand Prix of Poetry*, Macmillan, 1999. **Berlie Doherty**: David Higham Associates for "Dad" and "Grandpa" from *Walking on Air* by Berlie Doherty, HarperCollins. First published in *Another First Poetry Book*, OUP, 1987. **Carol Ann Duffy**: "There's a Dog" from *The Oldest Girl in the World* by Carol Ann Duffy, Faber and Faber Ltd., 2000. **Helen Dunmore**: "The Speak Mum Speaks" from *Snollygoster and Other Poems* by Helen Dunmore. Copyright © Helen Dunmore, first published by Scholastic Children's Books. All rights reserved. Reproduced by permission of Scholastic Ltd. **Richard Edwards**: the author for "Finding out about the Family" from *Teaching the Parrot* by Richard Edwards (Faber and Faber, 1986) and "Said Uncle" from *Whispers from a Wardrobe* by Richard Edwards (Lutterworth Press, 1987). **Willard R. Espy**: Louise Espy for "Skateboard" by Willard R. Espy. **Max Fatchen**: John Johnson (Authors' Agent) Limited for "My Dog" and "When Aunt Louisa Lit the Gas" by Max Fatchen from *Songs for My Dog and Other People* (Kestrel Books, 1980). Copyright © Max Fatchen 1980. **Aileen Fisher**: "Walking" from *Runny Days, Sunny Days* by Aileen Fisher. Copyright © 1958, 1986 Aileen Fisher. Used by permission of Marian Reiner for the author. **John Foster**: "My Gramp" and "There Are Four Chairs Round the Table" both copyright © John Foster from *Four O'Clock Friday* (Oxford University Press), included by permission of the author. **Martin Gardner**: the author for "Soap" by Martin Gardner from *Never Make Fun of a Turtle, My Son*, Simon and Schuster. **Jamila Gavin**: David Higham Associates for "They Chose Me" by Jamila Gavin from *Shimmy with My Granny*, Macdonald Young Books. **Nigel Gray**: David Higham Associates for "Fred" by Nigel Gray from *Poems About Families* (Wayland, 1994) and "My Cat" by Nigel Gray from *Another First Poetry Book* (Oxford University Press, 1998). **Eloise Greenfield**: "Grandma's Bones", "Mama" and "Missing Mama" from *Nathaniel Talking*, copyright © 1988 by Eloise Greenfield; "Flowers" from *Angels*, copyright © 1998 by Eloise Greenfield. Reprinted by permission of the Nancy Gallt Agency. "Nerissa" from *Night on Neighborhood Street* by Eloise Greenfield, copyright © 1991 by Eloise Greenfield, text. Used by permission of the Nancy Gallt Agency and Dial Books for Young Readers, an imprint of Penguin Putnam Inc. All rights reserved. **Nikki Grimes**: Copyright © "Little Sister" by Nikki Grimes. Copyright © "Remembering" by Nikki Grimes. First appeared in *Something on My Mind*, published by Dial Press. Reprinted by permission of Curtis Brown, Ltd. **Monica Gunning**: "Grandpa Milking Cows". Text copyright © 1993 by Monica Gunning from *Not a Copper Penny in Me House* by Monica Gunning. Published by Wordsong/Boyds Mill Press, Inc. Reprinted by permission. **Trevor Harvey**: the author for "The Painting Lesson" by Trevor Harvey from *The Usborne Book of Funny Poems* (Usborne, 1990). **Florence Parry Heide and Roxanne Heide Pierce**: "My Half" copyright © 1996 by Florence Parry Heide and Roxanne Heide Pierce. First appeared in *Oh Grow Up!* published by Orchard Books. Reprinted by permission of Curtis Brown, Ltd. **Dakari Hru**: "Tickle Tickle" by Dakari Hru from *In My Daddy's Arms I Am Tall*, Lee & Low Books, 1997. Permission arranged with Lee & Low Books, Inc., New York, NY 10016. **Langston Hughes**: "Madam's Christmas" from *The Collected Poems of Langston Hughes* by Langston Hughes, copyright © 1994 by The Estate of Langston Hughes. Used by permission of Alfred A. Knopf, a division of Random House, Inc., and by permission of David Higham Associates. **Ted Hughes**: "My Other Granny" from *Meet My Folks* by Ted Hughes, Faber and Faber Ltd, 1961. **James Hurley**: the author for "Greedy Dog" by James Hurley from *If You Should Meet a Crocodile*, Kaye & Ward, London. **Lynn Joseph**: "Mama" from *Coconut Kind of Day* by Lynn Joseph (Lothrop, Lee & Shepard Books), text copyright © 1990 by Lynn Joseph. Used by permission of HarperCollins Publishers. **Bobbi Katz**: "Cat Kisses" copyright © 1974 by Bobbi Katz, copyright © renewed 1996.

"My Brother" copyright © 1991 by Bobbi Katz, copyright © renewed 1997, published in *Could We Be Friends? Poems for Pals* by Bobbi Katz (New York: Mondo Publishing). "The Runaway" copyright © 1981 by Bobbi Katz. **Jackie Kay**: "New Baby" by Jackie Kay from *Dark as a Midnight Dream* (Evans, 1998). Reprinted by permission of PFD on behalf of Jackie Kay. Copyright © Jackie Kay. **X. J. Kennedy**: "Help!" copyright © 1975 by X. J. Kennedy. First appeared in *One Winter Night in August and Other Nonsense Jingles*, published by Margaret K. McElderry Books. Reprinted by permission of Curtis Brown, Ltd. **Jean Kenward**: the author for "Stepmother" by Jean Kenward from *All in the Family* (Oxford University Press, 1993). **Rudyard Kipling**: A P Watt on behalf of The National Trust for Places of Historical Interest or Natural Beauty for "Father, Mother, and Me" excerpted from "We and They" by Rudyard Kipling. **John Kitching**: the author for "Family Photo" from *Another Third Poetry Book* (Oxford University Press, 1988). **Lindamichellebaron**: the author for "Go Away" by Lindamichellebaron from *Families: Poems Celebrating the African-American Experience* (Boyds Mill Press, 1994). **Marian Lines**: the author for "Cinema" from *Tower Blocks: Poems of the City* by Marian Lines. Copyright © Marian Lines 1975. **Jean Little**: "I Told You So" and "Pearls", selections from *Hey World, Here I Am!* written by Jean Little and illustrated by Sue Truesdell, used by permission of Oxford University Press, HarperCollins Publishers and Kids Can Press Ltd., Toronto. Text copyright © 1986 by Jean Little. **Phyllis McGinley**: "Triolet Against Sisters", copyright © 1959 by Phyllis McGinley, from *Times Three* by Phyllis McGinley, published by Viking Penguin and Secker & Warburg. Used by permission of Viking Penguin, a division of Penguin Putnam Inc., and by permission of The Random House Group Limited. **Roger McGough**: "Tantrums" from *Pillow Talk* by Roger McGough (Viking, 1990). Copyright © Roger McGough, 1990. Reprinted by permission of PFD on behalf of Roger McGough. **Doug MacLeod**: Penguin Books Australia Limited for "Thank You, Dad, for Everything" from *The Fed-Up Family Album* by Doug MacLeod. **Colin McNaughton**: "Mum Is Having a Baby" from *Who's Been Sleeping in My Porridge?* copyright © 1990 Colin McNaughton. Reproduced by permission of Walker Books Limited, London. **Lindsay MacRae**: "The Auntie with a Kiss Like a Heat-Seeking Missile", "Family Tree", "Grandad's Lost His Glasses", "Will You Be My Family?" and "You Might As Well" from *How to Avoid Kissing Your Parents in Public* by Lindsay MacRae (Puffin 2000), copyright © Lindsay MacRae, 2000. Reproduced by permission of Penguin Books Ltd. **Michelle Magorian**: "Babies" copyright © Michelle Magorian 1989. Reproduced by permission of the author c/o Rogers, Coleridge & White Ltd., 20 Powis Mews, London W11 1JN. **Richard J. Margolis**: "Dinnertime", "His Dog" and "Teased" reprinted with the permission of Simon & Schuster Books for Young Readers, an imprint of Simon & Schuster Children's Publishing Division from *Secrets of a Small Brother* by Richard J. Margolis. Text copyright © 1984 Richard J. Margolis. **Margaret Mayo**: "Grandad's Shed" copyright © Margaret Mayo from *Hoddley Poddley: Favourite Rhymes and Verse*, compiled by Margaret Mayo, Orchard Books, 2001. **Tony Medina**: "When My Grandmother Died" from *DeShawn Days* by Tony Medina, Lee & Low Books, 2001. Permission arranged with Lee & Low Books Inc., New York, NY 10016. **Eve Merriam**: "Sometimes" from *Jamboree Rhymes for All Times* by Eve Merriam. Copyright © 1962, 1964, 1966, 1973, 1984 by Eve Merriam. All rights renewed and reserved. "Two People" from *A Word or Two with You* by Eve Merriam. Copyright © 1981 Eve Merriam. Both reprinted by permission of Marian Reiner. **Spike Milligan**: Spike Milligan Productions Limited for "My Sister Laura" from *Silly Verse for Kids* by Spike Milligan, Puffin 1968. **Tony Mitton**: David Higham Associates for "Growing" from *Plum* by Tony Mitton, Scholastic Children's Books and "Little Brother" from *I Want to Shout and Stamp About* by Tony Mitton, Hodder Wayland. **John Mole**: the author for "A Musical

permission of the author. **Danielle Sensier**: the author for "Breakfast" by Danielle Sensier from *Footprints on the Page* (Evans, 1998). **Shel Silverstein**: "My Sneaky Cousin" and "When I Was Your Age" from *Falling Up* by Shel Silverstein. Copyright © 1996 by Shel Silverstein. Used by permission of HarperCollins Publishers and Edite Kroll Literary Agency Inc. **Stevie Smith**: "Human Affection" by Stevie Smith, from *Collected Poems of Stevie Smith*, copyright © 1972 by Stevie Smith. Reprinted by permission of New Directions Publishing Corp and The Estate of James MacGibbon. **Sonya Sones**: "My Whole Family" from *Stop Pretending* by Sonya Sones. Used by permission of HarperCollins Publishers and Abner Stein. **Gary Soto**: "Ode to Family Photographs" from *Neighborhood Odes*, copyright © 1992 by Gary Soto, reprinted by permission of Harcourt, Inc. **Ian Souter**: "Kisses" copyright © Ian Souter, reprinted by permission of the author. **Pauline Stewart**: "Goodbye Granny", "Mountain Moon and Gold" and "Sauce" from *Singing Down the Breadfruit* by Pauline Stewart, published by Bodley Head. Used by permission of The Random House Group Limited. **Shirley Toulson**: David Higham Associates Limited for "Amber" copyright © Shirley Toulson, from *Over the Bridge* (Kestrel Books, 1981). **Kaye Umansky**: "Leaky Baby" by Kaye Umansky from *Shimmy with My Granny: Family Poems*, Macdonald Young Books, 1999. Copyright © Kaye Umansky. By kind permission of Kaye Umansky c/o Caroline Sheldon Literary Agency. **Judith Viorst**: "Mother Doesn't Want a Dog" by Judith Viorst. From *If I Were in Charge of the World and Other Worries* by Judith Viorst. Published by Atheneum Books for Young Readers, an imprint of Simon & Schuster Children's Publishing Division. Text copyright © 1981 Judith Viorst. Reprinted by permission of Simon & Schuster and Lescher & Lescher, Ltd. **Margaret Walker**: The University of Georgia Press on behalf of the author for "Lineage" from *This Is My Century: New and Collected Poems* by Margaret Walker (The University of Georgia Press). Copyright © Margaret Walker. **Jeanne Willis**: "Tea with Aunty Mabel" from *Toffee Pockets* by Jeanne Willis, published by Bodley Head. Used by permission of The Random House Group Limited. **Roger Woddis**: Joan Woddis for "Pity Your Parents" copyright © Roger Woddis 1991, from *Casting a Spell and Other Poems* (Orchard, 1991). **Janet S. Wong**: "Face It", "Quilt", "Sisters", "A Suitcase of Seaweed" and "When I Grow Up" reprinted with the permission of Margaret K. McElderry Books, an imprint of Simon & Schuster Children's Publishing Division, from *A Suitcase of Seaweed and Other Poems* by Janet S. Wong. Copyright © 1996 Janet S. Wong. **Kit Wright**: the author for "Our Hamster's Life" from *Rabbiting On* by Kit Wright (Fontana, 1978). Copyright © Kit Wright 1978. **Ray A. Young Bear**: "grandmother" from *Winter of the Salamander* by Ray A. Young Bear, HarperCollins. Reprinted by permission of the author. **Benjamin Zephaniah**: "I Luv Me Mudder" from *Wicked World* by Benjamin Zephaniah (Puffin, 2000). Text copyright © Benjamin Zephaniah. "Little Sister" from *Talking Turkeys* by Benjamin Zephaniah (Viking, 1994). Copyright © Benjamin Zephaniah, 1994. Reproduced by permission of Penguin Books Ltd.

Every effort has been made to obtain permission to reproduce copyright material, but there may have been cases where we have been unable to trace a copyright holder. The publisher would be happy to correct any omissions in future printings.